Gallivanting Through DOOM

By

Nobody Important

Cover Design: Benten Boychuk Boniface

www.nobodyimportant.ca

In human domestication, the information from the outside dream is conveyed to the inside world, creating our whole belief system … The domestication is so strong that at a certain point in life we no longer need anyone to domesticate us … we are an auto-domesticated animal.

Don Miguel Ruiz

When we live by a bunch of assumptions that we believe in fully but which are utter nonsense, we can call those assumptions delusions and can rightly conclude that we are psychotic. That would be our shared human situation. And to think that some people take it seriously?

Nobody Important

The entry point to the end of suffering is when you become conscious of the fact that you don't really know anything… We don't really want to admit that nobody really knows.

Adyashanti

Table of Contents

Introduction

The Oprah Interview (The Secret Bliss of Importance)

Why We Eventually Stumble and Break an Ankle on the "Ten Steps to Success" (None of the "How to Live" Maps Work)

To Find the Time to Write I Get Up at 2 AM (You Can't Have It All)

What Does the Fox Say? (Karma Revealed)

And You Thought You Could Control Your Feelings, Your Weight, and Your Obsession with Hockey (Control is a Bad Joke)

My Brilliant Analysis of The Sons of Anarchy (Family as the Ultimate Conspiracy)

Why Thanksgiving Should Be Cancelled (Why Family Ruins You for a Free Life)

Selling Water by The Bank of a River (Capitalism Rules Us All)

The Power of Yodeling (A Collaborative Study of Anxiety)

Hockey as a Somewhat Successful Coping Strategy (The Case for Climbing Mount DOOM)

Give Your Cows a Large Meadow to Graze In (Alien Invasion is Our Best Hope)

A Taste of the Fruit Bowl Experience (Going Beyond Difference)

Benedictus DOOMinus

Introduction

In the beginning there was something sudden, maybe a flash of divine lightning, which must have penetrated my brain, because the next thing I knew I had a finished manuscript inside of me and it had to be vomited out.

The only thing missing was a title. It seemed that there had been a delivery error and I would have to work that part out for myself.

It was hard. Like every brilliant writer, I wanted a title that would be catchy, yet elegant. I agonized. Sometimes elegance can be so elusive.

The title finally came to me and I'm sure you'll agree I succeeded in meeting my goals. I ask for your agreement because I'm honestly feeling a bit defensive. My editor, a grumpy old guy that I know exactly as well as I know myself, was slightly less than enthusiastic about *Gallivanting Through DOOM*. What a Debbie Downer he can be.

So, I know there's really no need to explain myself, but that's never stopped me before. "Gallivanting", as you well know, is a particular form of adventure that features very long steps, loud singing, winding trails that go up and down, sudden gleeful discoveries, and lots of old cheese and dill pickle sandwiches. And that is a description of my preferred style, for writing and living.

Don't you love the word "DOOMED". It's so precisely descriptive of your situation. Probably mine too, although maybe it will turn out that I'm special. But isn't it great to let DOOM blossom in all its fullness? Doesn't it just allow you to relax, like you were lying on your back on a donut-shaped floatie in a clear mountain lake on a warm summer afternoon? Really, fully, relax because you don't, for once, have to expend all that energy to pretend. You know, that things are fine, that we'll all be ok.

If that last bit about DOOM didn't resonate for you, I'm sorry, but I have to be straight and tell you that you need serious help. Fortunately, I can provide that.

In my catchy and elegant way, I will strip the Emperor and Empress bare of their invisible clothes. Boldly reveal how our everyday shared assumptions about how things are and how to live are absurd fabrications.

But, said all three of the friends who knew about my plans to write this book, you're just going to make everybody depressed. And the way things have been going, most people are already in a bad way.

I agree it's good to have friends, but really, sometimes they can be tedious. I have had to take time out from my prolific writing marathon to explain to them that DOOM doesn't have to be depressing. If you choose it instead of resent it. If you are curious about every deliciously DOOMED moment. It's a path to something wonderful.

I hate it when people roll their eyes, don't you?

Don't stay with that crowd. Join the happy DOOM movement. And come Gallivanting with me.

The Oprah Interview

Or

The Secret Bliss of Unimportance

If you knew me before it all changed, you would have had judgements. Well, I'm sure you'll still have some of those, but the judgements will be different. More like, is this guy just a whacko and undeserving of my attention. Less like, is this guy important enough to be worthy of my time. In the old days some of you might have decided I was sufficiently important to be given a chance, others definitely not. Today, however, importance is off the table. To be absolutely clear, I'm Nobody Important.

Before I tell you all about my unimportance, let me tell you a little about the former me who, like most everybody else, was in the business of gaining importance in the world. I do so to demonstrate that I wasn't a total slouch. Indeed, there were key moments of success that gave me hope. Like when I won a second-place ribbon at the Sunday School picnic obstacle race. Like when I was a starting forward for the Martin Monarch basketball team when we won the Southern Saskatchewan championship. Like when the guidance counselor told me that I was probably bright enough to go to university if I really applied myself. Like when I won a college contest for my poem *Materialism and Other Universes*. Like when I got a cool sign with my name over the door of the new office in the hospital psychology department. And I could go on.

There are some definite problems in trying to evaluate whether we are important and successful. For one thing, the criteria are murky. And the self-assessments tend to be unreliable from one day to the next. For example, yesterday when my partner Kerry's horoscope rightly foretold that she'd be feeling on top of the world she was sure that she was on the right track, making quality contributions to her family and friends, her workplace, and the world. Today's horoscope was different. And, oh, what a tale of woe!

Let's bring you into this discussion. Are you important? If you had to take a stand right now, could you say unequivocally that you are a success?

If you are absolutely certain, all the time, that you're a success and that everyone you know agrees that you are big-time important then you are a very unusual creature. Certainly deluded, but, more scarily, perhaps not even human. I don't want to get derailed right now by reflecting on the possibilities of alien invasion, but suffice it to say that we are all highly suspicious of you.

But enough about you. My own sordid situation is pretty clear, despite historical nods to success. Let me jump right in with the case against me.

As we are all very much aware, importance these days is primarily defined by social media reach. My track record here is sketchy. The truth is that I've never been on Facebook. Or

Twitter. Or other elaborations. I have no followers. I am not an influencer. I seem to have neglected things. Not out of principle or disapproval. Not due to technological incompetence. I could do it if it were absolutely necessary. More out of a lack of interest, or proper motivation. For example, yesterday my friend the groundhog visited in the backyard. I imagine that at least one of my friends might have liked to see her image on Facebook as a way of staying connected to me and my interests, but I was busy watching that low to the ground hustle, wondering what she was chewing on over by the fence. Stopping to photograph and post online didn't occur. Maybe I've just been too busy, and unwilling to take the time to participate properly in society?

I don't produce podcasts. I've watched some great podcasts and admire people who do them well. But they're clearly a lot of work. And I'd have to promote one if I made it. And that would mean that I'd have to compete with all those other wonderful people who have something important to say. And, somehow, I've just never made the effort.

On the upside, I made one entry into the blog I created for my work website. That was fun and maybe I'll do another some day. Kerry read it and she liked it. It gives me pleasure to give her pleasure.

I haven't been interviewed by Oprah. Nor have I turned down an invitation to be interviewed by her. There was a time when that was important to me, but I've mostly gotten over it.

I used to work as a researcher, and so I wrote and published quite a lot. While on the surface that might seem impressive, I need to tell you about the external review that was conducted. The reviewers noted that I was not publishing enough in the important journals, and was thus having only a moderate or less than moderate impact. Eventually I stopped writing articles for academic publication. A former friend suggested that I don't take criticism well.

I published three books, all intended to reach wide audiences. Back then I was willing to promote myself. I tried hard. I gave readings. I sought interviews. My mom saw me on early morning television once. But, alas, I received no offers to make the books into Hollywood movies or Netflix originals. And, sticking for now with the honesty theme, I don't recommend any of the books to you.

I am also a long- time meditator and teacher of meditation. Despite all of the effort over many years, I still consider myself very much a beginner. I have only two students left, both of whom have questionable judgement.

I am white, male, and over 65. I'll let that speak for itself.

I guess you can see that from any reasonable evaluation framework, I come up short of important.

Before moving things along, I want to elaborate on the problem of evaluative criteria. It seems that there is no point at which human (as opposed to alien) people feel able to rest confidently in their sense of success. There is always more to be had, somebody else to envy. And what success we have is always precarious.

Let's take an extreme example. Let's just say you were a rich and powerful person. And that you were so rich and powerful that you could decide to run for political office without any experience and that people would actually support your nomination. And let's say, however improbably, that you won and you were now the most important Who in Whoville. You'd think that under those conditions you would be able to just bask in the glory of it. Surely you would have proved to the whole world that you were as important as important can be. What need would there be to keep shouting your importance through social media. What need to be defensive, to lash out if any unimportant person happened to disagree with you. And yet …

How much success is enough?

So, you can see how this line of argument is in keeping with the truth that we are DOOMED. We seem to be wired to want to be important, yet it doesn't seem possible to fully achieve importance or keep what we gain. Silly us, we're forever banging our heads against the wall of ridiculous hope.

But here, right where self-harm is starting to seem like a reasonable path, there is one of those surprise discoveries that sometimes rewards the connoisseur of Gallivanting. Namely, that being nobody important has a whole other dimension, nothing to do with evaluation.

Embracing unimportance can release us from having to think about ourselves. When we play that "Get Out of Jail Free" card, and no longer have to tortuously consider our own worthiness all the time, we suddenly have all this room in our heads for everyone and everything else. It no longer seems like such a bizarre notion that we might take up the challenge of loving our neighbours like ourselves, as Jesus taught. Nor does the advice to be a person of "no rank", advocated by 9th century Zen Master Lin Chi, seem so crazy. We might now agree with him that there's no need for a fixed identity that we must cherish and promote, and we can go off Gallivanting in the "brisk and lively" way that he recommends. Could it be that striving for unimportance is some kind of recipe for freedom, a high spiritual path that moves us towards the truth that we are all expressions of the same vital life force, equally wondrous. Wow, that's a cool idea.

I hear the skeptics rolling their eyes. Again. Such a grating sound. They want to know if I think it's really possible to live in a place where self-concern and importance do a disappearing act?

What, you expect me to have all the answers? I don't know what's possible. I do know that Bliss has been visiting more often as I get less and less important. But, my goodness, it's not an easy path. Some days I want to just give up and go ahead and send my writing off to a literary agent and get a big contract and make a ton of money and let Oprah interview me and be a household name everywhere. It would be so much easier than this ongoing effort to keep turning towards unimportance.

For example, as I write this sentence thoughts are circling through my mind about how my presentation of this topic and thus my self may be perceived. Will I be seen as a moralistic authoritarian, trying to appear to rise above petty human concerns, and criticizing everyone who falls prey to self interest? That would be unfortunate. Or will I be seen as a crusty old loser with axes to grind who's just trying to find a silver lining in a pig's ear? That would also be unfortunate. But these concerns reflect perilous desires to be somebody who will be relevant and understood and, yes, important. You can see the difficult track of this exploration. That despite my efforts to not take seriously my own importance, these considerations arise all the time, call to me, seduce me towards particular investments in self presentation. Am I willing to resist the waves of self-importance and keep jumping into our shared unimportance?

Good question.

Why We Eventually Stumble and Break an Ankle on the "Ten Steps to Success"

Or

None of the "How to Live" Maps Work

The world is full to the rim with templates or maps for how to be successful, how to be happy, how to be a good parent, how to find love. Etcetera. The idea of a map that could show us how to get where we want to go has tons of traction. Just look at Google Maps and MapQuest! But we'd also like to avoid the kind of thing that happened when I tried to find the rental cottage last summer using the map app. Too many of us have found ourselves at the end of that dirt road, looking out over acres of swamp, wondering how we ended up like this.

So, is it too much to hope for a decent map to show us how to live? Probably, but let's investigate. I'll bring my finely honed skills as a former research scientist to this important undertaking. In the process, we will look at a couple of really compelling maps for life, provided by very high profile, credible characters: God and Tony Robbins. I was unsure which of these characters to mention first, but decided to go in historical order. God, after all, got there pretty early on and arguably has the longest track record with His/Her/Their map.

So, the Ten Commandments is a first-rate example of a map for how humans can live successfully, dictated by God. Success from this perspective would seem to be equated with receiving divine approval and possibly a pass into heaven.

I'm not going to insult your intelligence by writing out all of the Ten Commandments. I assume you know them by heart.

But let me stop right there and situate myself in this writing and acknowledge my own cultural and religious biases.

You see, I grew up in a neighbourhood in a town at a time where there seemed to be only one way of viewing things, and where there was only one type of person doing the viewing. Cultural diversity was expressed by the single Chinese restaurant. I didn't hear the word homosexuality (although I guess it's possible that I heard it and just repressed it) until I hit high school. As for religion, there was some diversity in town. There were Baptists, like us. And then there were less approved folk, like Presbyterians, Methodists, Lutherans, and Anglicans. What you had to be most careful of was the Catholics, because it was unclear whether they might just be heathens in disguise. Having never met a real-life heathen, this was of considerable interest to my six-year-old self. But as Grandma explained, all those sculptures in their churches, especially the ones with blood on them, amounted to a rude violation of one of the Ten Commandments, that you not create "graven images", not worship idols or figures. Grandma was one of the most important supporters in my early life, helping me to read a map properly.

Aside from the lack of diversity, things were generally what you could call tamped down where I grew up. One day my younger brother heard some really bad kid say the "F" word at school and, fool that he was, decided to try it out at home. My dad had his belt out and part way into a good swing before our cries of innocence provoked an unusual restraint. Given that we didn't know we were sinning, he took the time to explain things to us. So it was that we learned that "fucking" had to do with what dogs did to each other sometimes. Which left both my brother and I with a new wariness about dogs, that there might be worse things than being bitten.

So, all of this to say that you might want to proactively forgive me. It has taken me a lot of time and effort to climb part way out of the pit of ignorance that I grew up in, and some days it's like the mud on the sides of the pit give way and I'm right back at the bottom, thinking, and, Lord help me, sometimes saying or writing things that are profoundly stupid.

When I was about eight my Grandma made a deal with me. If I could memorize the Ten Commandments, she would buy me a present of my choosing (if she could afford it). I was quick to agree. My choice for a present was a pellet rifle. Now you might ask why I would want a gun, not being American. Well, it's pretty obvious. It was because I was an eight-year-old boy. Clear enough?

Back then, I had no idea that there could be alternate choices for gender socialization much less gender identity or the wild freedom of gender fluidity. I'm tempted to say that I was a victim of my limited conditioning but that might make me seem like a real wuss.

Grandma was a bit taken aback by my request, mainly because it seemed there was some stickiness vis-a-vis another of the Commandments, "though shalt not kill". She quickly rallied, saying that I could have the gun if I promised not to kill with it. I agreed, but of course, being an eight-year-old boy, I was unable (maybe even unwilling) to live up to my promise to be good. Later, when I shot the gopher and watched her horrible writhing death it came as a surprise to me to realize that God was a lot smarter than I'd been allowing for.

So now, as I continue to follow the map of "ten steps to write successfully", I ask you dear reader to turn your mind to the next logical consideration. Namely, the problem of interpretation. Put simply, any time we write something down people are going to have a whole bunch of different ideas about what we really mean. Like when Tony Robbins stated that the first step to success is "Raise Your Standards". The moment he made that bold statement he opened himself up to a world of grief. Like, what the heck does it mean? Is he saying that we're all a bunch of complacent nits? Is he promoting endless personal growth or just the possibility of moving up in the world a bit? Does he have a particular type of standard that we should all aspire to? Each

17

reader brings a particular perspective, and looks at the statement through the glasses of their past experience and current self-interest. In other words, we can hardly help from twisting whatever truths that come our way to match our own perverted view of things.

What might I do with the prospect of "raising my standards"? The first thing that comes to mind is reducing my consumption of take-out roti, thereby following new and promising standards of moral dietary behaviour.

Ok, to be fair to Tony Robbins he does do quite a bit of explicating about each of his 50 top steps to success. Which is a bit of a mixed blessing, because that's a lot of verbiage to inhale even if it does help to clarify things.

God could have benefited from studying Tony's approach, or from reading a book on how to write for success. Case in point, the commandment, Thou Shall Not Kill. He/She/Them really should have been more specific about what is intended here as lack of clarity has created no end of mess. Indeed, when as part of my scientific research into this matter I Googled the Ten Commandments I discovered that there is a raging controversy over whether the correct translation and/or interpretation should be Thou Shalt Not Murder. Now there's a big difference, don't you think, between kill and murder. And if he meant murder, well, that might (depending on your interpretation of murder) be a huge relief for a lot of people. Including hunters, meat-eaters, soldiers, pest removers, literary agents, etc. But if kill is the authoritative term, then we're all in a world of trouble, including the Jain monks whose commitment to nonviolence involves using peacock-feather dusters to sweep the ground where they walk to avoid killing any life-forms.

So, what is my point here? It's really not to say that "Thou Shalt Not Kill" is a ridiculous guideline. Indeed, it seems to me to point at an important sensitivity to unnecessary harm. And a recognition of our interconnectedness with everyone and everything. I want to cultivate that sensitivity and experience our connectedness. My point is that I could be the Darth Vader of my neighbourhood and still find a way to interpret God's commandment to somehow support my treacherous ways. The commandment is not a fixed thing that can be nailed down once and for all, interpreted the same way by all of us. Nothing is.

The other main point is that whatever map we turn to for guidance about how to live will sometimes be terribly wrong. In exploring this assertion, let's give Tony Robbins his turn. For argument's sake, let's just say that his exhortation to "Raise Your Standards" is a genuine feature of success for many people. But Tony, there are some people for whom this is the worst suggestion possible. Namely those whose impossible standards for themselves already cause them suffering.

Recently, my daughter Benten had to produce a video for her Chemistry course, showing a visual representation of various compounds and talking the viewer through her understanding of possible chemical reactions. The video was due the next day. There was a test that also needed to be studied for. She'd been hemming and hawing about the best way to shoot the video, whether or not she'd gotten the information right, and of course not wanting to appear on video so that she might be judged by others. It was unclear whether her trajectory towards adulthood might be permanently stopped right here, unable to move beyond this moment of stuckness. Now, if my partner Kerry had been following Tony Robbins' "steps for success" she probably would have suggested that Benten raise her standards to the next level, maybe do a yet better job before submitting. You know, pour some more cement around her feet. Instead, she urged something to the effect of "would you just get off your butt and finish this with what you've got because there's other work to do." Despite the possible value of Tony's map for success, and not just because I believe in parents supporting each other wherever possible in their interactions with kids, I was basically, "heck yeah" about Kerry's intervention.

That's a little example of how raising standards can go wrong. But how about all those perfectionists who take forever to finish their tax returns and only finally complete them after they're assessed for their second penalty. Maybe they should just have higher standards before they take the final step? And how about the eating disorder people, who look at their wasting bodies in the mirror and see only one thing, FAT. What we really don't need in that situation is higher standards of thinness.

Ok, I know it seems that I'm picking on Tony. But it wouldn't matter who I chose, or what their "key to success", we'd nevertheless find that it's sometimes a really bad idea.

For example, there's the "Law of Attraction", which has many avid followers, the basic idea being that positive or negative thoughts bring positive or negative experiences. The formula for success is think positively, not negatively. Sounds good. Very actionable. And yet, in my twenty years of working as a psychologist in a cancer hospital I met a lot of very positive people who had really crummy outcomes. Thus, clearly not a sure thing. To suggest it is a "law" means that those dead people were all losers, unable to follow simple instructions. Do you think, then, that it might be a problem to suggest to ill people that the absolute key to success is positivity?

And then there's me, connoisseur of DOOM, and yet living the high life, rolling in an orgy of wealth from the royalties from my writing. Take that, Law of Attraction!

Finally, circling back to God, how could we argue with advice from such an exalted character. Surely a commandment from God can't ever be wrong. Just consider, Honour thy father and mother. How could that ever be a bad idea? (Cue: that was a joke). Have you met some of the mothers and fathers that I've met? I'm a psychologist. I could tell you stories.

I'm guessing that by now you must be bitterly disappointed. We've all been looking, in books and movies and Facebook and obituaries, for the right way to live, and the ultimate map to show the way. And it turns out, as proven by my unassailable logic, that we can't rely on any of these maps or any of the mapmakers, at least not fully. And that sucks.

But in this DOOMED uncertain situation, the world over the next hill is ours to discover, and we'll get to choose whether to go left or right, into the forest or along the lake's edge.

And which song to sing next.

To Find the Time to Write I Get Up at 2 AM

Or

You Can't Have It All

Have you ever been in therapy? If not, you might have fantasies about a warm, unconditionally supportive person who is more interested in you than anyone has ever been before. So, when someone says to you, "maybe you should talk to someone about that", if you're able to ignore that old tape in your head that goes, "but I am perfectly capable of taking care of myself", you might really look forward to time spent with someone who gets you but nevertheless still likes you.

If you have actually been in therapy, however, you know that therapists can be really annoying.

Like my therapist Ruby (name changed to protect my survival). Oh yes, she could be supportive. And she helped me, I do admit. I am slightly less of a problem than I used to be. I think a 360-degree assessment with friends and family might support that bold statement. Maybe. But, was she annoying? Absolutely.

I am a psychologist. I haven't always been one, and as part of my training I learned that the predominant emphasis in therapy should be on client experience, and that clients should, for the most part, be supported to come to their own insights and breakthroughs. Now this is a difficult thing to achieve, as we all have this tendency to give advice because we believe that we know the right way to live, and that may be especially true of therapists because of all the insights they gain in attending university.

Now most therapists come to little agreements with themselves about when it is ok to insert gems of wisdom that they have come to believe and cherish. In moderation, just to be helpful, as an adjunctive method to support their clients' own process.

> Sidebar: I have to say that insurance-funded brief therapy has been changing the expectation, and more and more therapists feel like they might as well tell clients everything they know because they only have a few sessions before the funding runs out and the clients really need help right now to stop screwing up.

Anyway, as I was saying about Ruby's annoyingness, she had selected some gems for transmission. And periodically she'd trot them out for my edification. My suspicion is that she probably exceeded the admissible number of gems per session but I never complained to her Regulatory College. If she knew about that decision to restrain my right to complain, she would surely have found a way to bring me around to an insight that I was once again avoiding direct action. That I would be more likely to take the passively aggressive route and maybe write about my complaint years later rather than risk conflict. But that's not the type of annoying I want to highlight here.

One of her favourite sayings was, "You can have anything you want, but you can't have everything". She would smile just a little bit when she said it. While I would smile in return, reaching towards that elusive good patient status, inside I'd be slightly annoyed. Part of it was her tone, that almost nauseating mixture of empathetic understanding, breathtaking smugness, and hardcore pleasure in my pain. Regarding the latter, in my humble professionally valid opinion, compared to therapists, dominatrices are rank amateurs in the dark arts of pleasure/pain exploration.

Annoyed. Like, what a lot of baloney! I can have anything I want. Really? On what back of what cereal box did you read that? Have you been binge watching old Rocky movies on your weekends? Were you really listening when you took my history in our first session? Wanted my dad to spend time with me. No. Wanted to be the star of my high school basketball team. No. Wanted to be most popular kid at the dance. No. Wanted to be a researcher superstar. No. Wanted to sell many copies of my book. No. Wanted to be invited by Oprah for an interview. No.

You get the idea. So, if I said right now that what I really wanted was to be a great actor the Ruby that still infests my brain might say. "Good, it's yours". And then she might add, "But do you really want it?" And this is where annoyance starts to slide towards rage. The implication would be that all my past failures might have had something to do with insufficient wanting, substandard commitment. That I'm really a passive-aggressive, inadequately motivated, useless nit.

Ok, that was being unfair to Ruby. What she would want to be pointing out is that if I want to be a great actor it would require much of me. Yes, I would have to "really" want it. And here is where the second part of her gem would re-emerge. "But you can't have it all." In other words, if it were ever to be achievable, I would have to pay a cost. Many costs.

This is where my considerable self-awareness comes in handy. I recognize that my rage in reaction to being told that I can't have it all is multiply determined. Partly, I just don't like being told how things are. As in, "you don't know it all dad!", whispered quietly into my pillow at night just to be safe. You'd think school would have taken care of this resistance to authority for me. But it didn't. Like all serious conspiracy theorists, I just can't fully overcome my perpetual teenage rebellion against any official version of anything. You know, you're all trying to make me kneel down and accept your undeserved authority.

But, closer to the core of the problem, I really don't like when other people are right when they tell me how I should think and live. You know how that can be. "You should be more grateful, maybe make time to write in your gratitude journal every day". Bugger off. "You should pay more attention to your grooming". Go away. "

But they are right. Gratitude is a great feeling to have. I feel it a lot. And I want to evoke it more every day. Just don't tell me to do it. Ok? And about the grooming, yeah, yeah, I get it, but being a pandemic and all …

So, we've gotten close to understanding the central complex that explains why I found Ruby so annoying back then and still fantasize about texting her to tell her so. It's because it's true that I can't have everything I want. None of us can.

Of course, I understand. It is possible that you're a special case. That your unique configuration of skills and character make it possible to balance all those competing interests and needs in an elegant way. I know. Let me soothe you. Just because I've been working as a therapist for more than 30 years and never seen an elegant demonstration of trying to have it all doesn't mean that you're not really special and won't achieve success. There, there.

Now that you've calmed a bit, let me provide some very scientific examples of "trying to have it all" pathology.

I have a neighbour, the professor living in the bungalow with the yellow door and the weed-infested lawn. I'll call him Peter to protect his identity. For quite a few years, from even before the pandemic, we made a habit of stopping to chat for a few minutes in a socially distant kind of way, whenever we were both outside doing stuff. When I first met him, Peter was already well on his way to a distinguished academic career. Over the years of our curbside meetings, he soared from one success to the next. The first research grants multiplied into many grants. Collaborations with local colleagues morphed into massive international studies.

27

Instead of the few graduate students that initially sought him out he soon had an army of eager, needy people to advise. Invitations to speak increased exponentially. He was approached to consult with government. Seduced by private industry to accept lucrative contracts. He told me about it all. And about how much he loved his high-flying life.

Once in a while, being a thoughtful and caring neighbour, I would ask whether he ever felt overwhelmed by his many projects. I even tried out a gentle version of Ruby's gem on him, "Boy oh boy, that sounds like a lot. Maybe just keep an eye out for if it gets to be too much". But he would reassure me that everything was fine.

Eventually, and inevitably, the cracks started to show. One afternoon when I was trying to get my groceries from the car into the house, he launched into a long rant about efficiency. And how, being a scientist, he had broken down his week into 15-minute segments and recorded how he spent his time. In the end he concluded that he was pretty damn efficient. Not much room to improve, except maybe the occasional Sunday evening when he was prone to collapsing into Netflix oblivion and, of course, the unnecessary chats with neighbours.

Another time, raking the yard took way too long because I was interrupted by Peter's prolonged tirade about setting priorities. He regaled me with his description of his reflective process and then, how, in the end, he decided everything he was involved with was a high priority that he wasn't willing to give up. Meanwhile, week after week he was becoming yet more successful and more requests poured in.

A crisis careened into sight when he decided on two new big projects. The comprehensive podcast series that would be definitive for his field. And his long-delayed desire to start dating again. He was passionate about both undertakings, boldly announcing them when I stepped onto the porch to retrieve my mail.

Time passed. It seemed I was seeing less of Peter, which I must say wasn't a huge disappointment. But on a rainy day the following spring he told me over our precariously leaning fence that he'd managed to just that week get his first Podcast interview scheduled. And that although he'd set up his online dating profile, he was waiting for an opening in his schedule to make an initial contact.

Months passed until I saw Peter again and when I spied him out the front window, he didn't look so good, dramatically exceeding the normal grooming slippage for middle aged men during a pandemic. You know, bedroom slippers in the snow kind of slippage.

That was my last sighting. Things have been quiet next door. I feel a bit lost and helpless. What do you think I should do?

Let me provide one other example, which will demonstrate how trying to have it all is not just a problem for men. This example is taken from the archives of no less an important historical figure than Sigmund Freud. As you undoubtedly know, Sigmund kept detailed records of his meetings and wrote many of his clients up as case studies. Unless you're a scholar of the history of psychoanalysis you probably don't know about Judith, whose presenting problem was anger management.

> Sidebar: When I asked Kerry to read a draft of this part, she got very confused and upset because she couldn't tell if I was being historically accurate in my rendering. So, for all you detail-obsessed worry warts, Sigmund did write case studies but Judith was actually not a client, and, if she were, he would have been way out of his depth.

Judith came to her meetings with Sigmund prepared. She had a list of issues to cover. This list was inevitably lengthy because it included: challenges that came with being a corporate vice-president and with her volunteer work on various boards, communicating with her sometimes difficult and romantically aloof spouse, mothering her 3 wonderful, but often exasperating, children, the politics of extended family dinners that she inevitably had to organize, the arguments she had at her periodic women's retreats, and so on. She expected to cover all the issues she identified. She made good eye contact while she talked to Sigmund, ("a tad intense" he wrote in his notes), for up to 3 minutes at a time. Then she would check her watch to make sure

30

they were moving at an appropriate pace. She wanted Sigmund's advice about how to fix each problem that she raised. She provided him with feedback about her assessment of the likely benefit of each suggestion he provided. She especially wanted to know how he would measure her progress to ensure that her goals were being met and that she wasn't wasting her time. At the end of each session, she wanted to know how Sigmund saw their work progressing. She double-checked her next appointment time, reminding him to send her the Zoom link in advance.

Most commentators on the Judith case have limited their discussion to the ways in which trying to have it all contributed to a serious neurotic disorder, a hypervigilant monitoring that was necessitated by attempts to cover so many bases all at once. But what has been overlooked is how this case study contributed significantly to Sigmund's development of the notion of countertransference. I don't want to seem condescending, but just in case you've forgotten, let me remind you that countertransference is a reaction whereby therapists come to experience their clients' feelings as if they were their own.

Being very self-aware, Sigmund noticed that since starting his therapeutic work with Judith, once every couple of weeks he would drink a bottle of wine, throw his shoes at his wife, and send his adult kids to bed without a story. When his son the banker and his daughter, mother of six, complained about his unseemly behaviour he surmised that he was feeling and acting as if he were Judith. Ta da! Sigmund had an insight! Countertransference was a key scientific discovery, probably comparable in importance to the discovery of insulin.

I believe I have now provided ample evidence for how trying to have everything creates problems for people. And the most disturbing implication from this finding is that we can't ultimately be satisfied, can't ever get enough to fill the hole. Talk about your inconvenient truth! How will you Gallivant through that, you ask?

One long stride after another.

Let's not stop now just because we don't know where we're going and might not ever arrive in the Land of Satisfaction.

Who said that hole had to be filled anyway?

What Does the Fox Say?

Or

Karma Revealed

As I turn to face into the topic of karma, a wave of anxiety crests and splashes all over me. Karma, as you undoubtedly know, comes to us most directly from Eastern spiritual traditions. And I have a long and intimate connection with one such tradition, namely Buddhism. Engagement with meditation and the mystical path within Buddhism, has made life much more vivid and rich for me, freed me in wildly wonderful ways. I'm deadly serious! So, the last thing I want to do is cast aspersions on this tradition, make fun of it in a manner that might lead my multitudinous readers to think that I think it's all just gonzo silliness.

Besides which, religions have these warnings against speaking out of turn. In the Buddhist Precepts practitioners are cautioned to "not slander the Dharma". Similarly, in the Ten Commandments there is, "Thou shalt not take the Lord's name in vain". In short, don't step out of line. Or perhaps, don't make too much fun.

So, you can see why I'm anxious. I have to walk a very careful line, daring to introduce a dollop of levity into the reality of our prevailing DOOM while trying to avoid a major screw-up that will get me punished and lead me to feel really bad and deservedly so.

About karma. Deep breath. It's a very profound, complicated, and mysterious teaching. I'll try to walk you through it but you might want to pop one of your ADHD pills first. If you get lost, feel free to send me an email requesting clarification.

Here goes.

Karma: "Actions have consequences".

Wow. No wonder we couldn't figure that out all on our own here in the West.

Ok, let's do a little check-in. Am I out of line? Maybe too flippant about the serious message of karma? Too irreverent altogether about religion?

Thanks, Clara, for your thoughtful email. I agree I could maybe tone things down a bit. And you're probably right that I should clarify how my privileged position as a white male is problematic. And that my engagement with Buddhism may amount to cultural appropriation. Frank, I understand that you think Buddhists are just heathens and should burn in Hell but my insights may also be relevant for other traditions. Marigold, I am not intending to incite hate towards people with ADHD, but, really, if you're going to write critiques could you at least finish your sentences? Alistair, Jeremy, Claude and Suzanne, there's no need to SHOUT.

Sidebar: Did you hear the one about the Zen priest, the Baptist minister and the Sufi master who walk into a bar ....?

In the lineage of Zen Buddhism that I initially trained in, there is a book of stories (also called koans) that practitioners study after they've had a breakthrough experience. The first story in the first book is about karma. An old monk who'd seen deeply into the nature of his own mind, and thus experienced a new sense of freedom, was asked whether an enlightened person could fall under the chain of cause and effect (i.e., the law of karma). He answered, "No." Which was clearly the wrong (or incomplete) answer, because he was immediately transformed into a fox and had 500 subsequent rebirths as a fox. In the story, he was finally released from his fox's body when he gave a new answer, that nobody, however enlightened, should ever ignore the law of karma. Whenever we try to avoid how our actions have consequences, trouble will come calling.

The implications of this story reverberate for me these days. For example, when Kerry and I go on our morning walk along the edge of the ravine that goes down to Lake Ontario we often see a fox trotting along, looking for breakfast. Sometimes I call out, "Don't ignore karma", just in case he's another of those old monks that got carried away by his insight, but now eager to find a way back to the monastery. So far, the foxes have all ignored me. I'm wondering if they're just having too good a time in their exile from the shenanigans of human society.

35

So, we've established that karma is important and shouldn't be ignored. Yet, wouldn't you know it, we ignore it all the time. For example,

- "It won't hurt to have one more donut."
- "My boss will thank me for my constructive criticism."
- "It's just a little harmless flirting."
- "Surely it's just smart business to borrow money to make money."
- "If I keep telling that boy to try harder, I'm sure he'll try harder."
- "The odds have got to turn in my favour eventually. I'll put it all on Lucky Lucy to win."

So, we all know that a lot of people, including a lot of Buddhists, have a belief in reincarnation, or rebirth. Me, not so much, but I'm willing to entertain it as a working hypothesis. Anyway, did you know that there is a detailed process for how people think rebirth happens? And that this process is very much tied up with karma? In the time leading up to death, before all the stuff that goes on in the bardos (in-between states) before rebirth, it's seen to be important, if at all possible, to remain alert. That's because the very last thought or image that you have can influence the conditions for your next life. It's like it gives you a boost in a particular direction. A karmic boost. So, for example, if you've been a sincere meditator all your life and your last thought is of wanting to meditate more, maybe for your next life you'll find yourself devout Buddhist parents in a valley in Tibet. Something like that.

So, if you know someone on their deathbed, and you know something about what they might want for a future life maybe you can find ways to support that intention. Like my dying friend Jonathan. Knowing about his desire to be a more sincere spiritual practitioner next time around, but also knowing about his tumultuous, scattergun relationship history, I intervened and asked the graceful nurse with the lovely almond eyes to wait just a minute before she went into his room. Unfortunately, she wasn't one of those special nurses who will listen to reason, and so in she went. Jonathan looked longingly into her eyes. She looked back. His last words before he died, "oh no, not again".

Now if that were a true story, I would still be feeling my guilt at not intervening effectively. As it is, my guilt is limited to the possible damage of my questionable wit on attractive, bull-headed nurses everywhere, Tibetans trying to free themselves from traditional stereotypes, and my friend Jonathan's grieving parents.

At least you now have a thorough-going understanding of karma. It's all rather sobering, isn't it, that we don't just get a free pass to do what we want and never have to pay the price. DOOMED to such an unfair weight of responsibility.

I don't know how I'll be able to enjoy eating my sandwiches when we take our next break.

And You Thought You Could Control Your Feelings, Your Weight, and Your Obsession with Hockey

Or

Control is a Bad Joke

Have you ever woken in the middle of the night in a total state of panic? Well, it happened to me last night. At first, I wasn't sure what the panic was about but after a lot of abdominal breathing and intensive self examination, I discovered that I was petrified that I might have seriously misled my readers in the previous chapter on karma.

> Sidebar: This writing business is tricky, especially when dealing with such seminal matters as DOOM. You know, being seen as an expert and people taking in what I write and immediately seeing the truth of it and then acting on it and changing their whole lives. Wow, it's a bit scary to have all that power.

I didn't mislead readers with my definition of karma. Actions do have consequences. And the point I made about people tending to be too cavalier about karma was certainly accurate. But what I failed to do was warn you about an obvious, frequently made leap of inaccurate reasoning. Namely, that just because actions have consequences that are sometimes pretty predictable it doesn't mean that you can control your life by acting properly. My goodness, it would be pure folly if you took what I was saying to mean that making "excellent" choices would guarantee you a charmed life. Have you not heard of chaos theory?

I do hope that this message has reached you in time to prevent serious harm.

Speaking of harm, I'm sure you know that writers all take an oath to avoid harm at all costs, to put readers' well being ahead of their own. And you probably also know, writers who try to be funny have to take extra steps, as prescribed by their Regulatory College. Not only must they take the oath to not harm, but have to chant it five thousand times while doing prostrations before a statue of the god Ethics, represented as a severe looking, uncompromising man carrying a sledgehammer. This expectation to undertake extra diligence is because humorists find it so much harder than ordinary writers to avoid harm, walking a razor's edge between glee and pain. Walking that line is especially challenging because people who think they're funny are genetically predisposed to a neuro-atypical confusion between the two experiences.

You probably know what's going to come next. Yes, you're right. Of course, there is a serious problem in obtaining compliance to the Regulatory College's guidelines for humorists. Last I checked there was a seven-year backlog in disciplinary cases to be heard by the Board. By my figuring, the odds are about even as to whether I'll be dead before I have to defend myself.

It would be understandable if you thought that my non-compliance in paying homage to Ethics is because of my commitment to individual freedoms, But, no, it's not because I think "anything goes" with humor. It's just that I don't like to be told what to do, even when Ethics is right. Don't tell me that it's ok to tell this kind of joke but not that kind of joke. You know, like, "feel free to punch up but not down". I'll figure it out. Do it my own way, using my experience to guide me. Like when I was feeling a lot of pain about a family member killing himself. And there was a wave of jokes about suicide. I didn't need an ethicist (an earthly emissary of the god Ethics) to tell me how to think about that. In one way, I wished I could see the lightness in it. But I couldn't. So, I try to think about other people the same way, leaning into their pain to try and assess the degree of damage that being, or trying to be, funny might have. I know I get it wrong sometimes. So does Ethics. Sorry on behalf of both of us.

Despite best efforts to avoid inflicting unnecessary pain, it's ultimately quite hopeless. After all, we're all hauling a truck load of pain, whether we are aware of it or not, and who knows when an offhand witticism might tap into the motherload for any of us. It's ultimately out of my control. Just like everything else. Which is how I got started on this tangent if I remember correctly.

Continuing with our theme of control, have you heard of something called "cognitive behavioral therapy"? It's a short-term approach to therapy that is very popular, especially among insurance companies and the 83% of psychologists who score more than two standard deviations above the norm on the need for control scale. The premise is that if you control your thoughts, you can fully control your feelings and your life. Hoo, hoo, that's a good one! They really should have to undertake the College's protocol for funny people. Anyway, various strategies are promoted to control thoughts, including critically evaluating your negative, catastrophic thoughts so that you can challenge them rationally and replace them eventually with alternative thoughts. So, for example, if you were afraid that a little levity might cause serious harm you can challenge that belief. Like, "has anyone ever died from your wit?" Or "what's the likelihood that everyone that you love will reject you permanently and throw you out on the street if your joke is tasteless?" And so on.

I must admit that I sometimes fall prey to catastrophic thinking. And just as the cognitive-behaviorists would have it, my careful evaluation of those thoughts usually leaves me feeling pretty silly. Like this morning, after all that writing about Buddhism and karma yesterday, I admit I was still shocked at the sight of the Buddhist monks picketing in front of my house, carrying placards like, "Go on a Silent Retreat Forever", "Your Last Life Must Have Been a Doozy", and "The Fox Says Your Karma Sucks". But I was also relieved because that was so much less catastrophic than I'd imagined. After all, I'm still here to be able to tell you about it.

Is it really necessary to lay out why control is a bad joke? I'd have thought not, but last night my daughter Benten told me she would win our after-dinner card game if she believed in herself. (Note: I destroyed her and continue as the reigning Uno champ). But her belief about control was right up there with thinking you won't get cancer if you exercise regularly and cut down on your drinking. And my deluded belief that digging the weeds out of the front garden would mean they were gone for good. Always possible. Maybe a little karmic boost in the right direction. But control?! Let's not kid ourselves.

> Sidebar: Gerard, although you can't guarantee control over your health, please don't use this argument as an excuse to start back up with that beer and sausages habit.

It is with some trepidation that I'm going to further pursue my thesis about the folly of control. I really hate to be pulling this proverbial rug out from under our feet. After all, how can we go on if we don't feel in control, or at least that control is possible? Are we not then DOOMED to helplessness?

Yes, pretty much so. But I know some good blues tunes. And we can still do our best.

But let me proceed by provoking another of our gods, namely Science. As you all know, Science's preferred weapon is the scientific method. To wield that weapon is to predict and control.

When I was a budding social scientist in pursuit of a Master's degree, I had to use the scientific method to conduct research that would show the impact of a specific variable. The way that you do that is to control all other variables except the one you're interested in. You know, hold them all still without even the slightest wavering in the breeze so that you will know that whatever change you observe will be due only to the variable you are interested in and manipulating. This seemed to me a very elegant method and I was sure I would always be a follower of Science.

I had some fascinating ideas for a research project. One by one, these were rejected by my supervisor until it became clear that he wanted me to undertake a study in his area of expertise. It seemed I didn't have as much control as I'd imagined. But I had learned what it takes to be a successful student. And, so, we moved forward with a study of "prosocial modeling". The idea being that if human beings see other human beings acting in a helpful "prosocial" way they are more likely to be helpful themselves.

I was going to compare two groups of daycare kids. One group would see a video of an adult taking care of a "sick" child, showing affection, taking temperature, etc. The other group would see a different video of an adult playing with stuffed animals. Later children from both groups would be taken, one at a time, into a room to play with an older child. The play was introduced as a chance to take care of a sick boy. Rates of helping behaviour were recorded, and any differences would be due to the impact of the modeling the kids had watched on video.

Still with me? Anyway, the success of this study depended on keeping everything besides the video-watching variable the same for both groups. Pretty straightforward? What could go wrong?

Here's a sampling. We failed to consider that some kids would participate before their afternoon nap and some after and that that would have a bearing on crankiness and the likelihood of "non-helping" behaviour. Some of the kids were unable to attend fully to the video, either because they'd forgotten their medication or were used to more stimulating, action-packed shows. One of the boys watching the helping video was the son of a doctor and kept interrupting to tell the other kids in his group how great his mom was. A shy little girl had a sick cat at home and began to cry when asked to take care of the sick boy. The child playing the sick role became more and more surly as the afternoon progressed and he realized that he had the researcher (me) over a barrel and could ask for candy and money to ensure his ongoing compliance. His mother, a friend of mine, decided she needed to intervene and talk to her son about his acting skills, so that part way through the day he began to act as if he was not just sick but dying painfully, very dramatically.

I could go on. It was a mess. All kinds of variables were moving all over the place.

Later, when I presented my study to a group of professors, they were enthusiastic. But my supervisor winked when he stated that my findings (that there was no difference in prosocial behaviour between the two video-watching groups) were fully supported by Science.

So, it seems that even the god Science is in on the great deception, refusing to acknowledge that control is just a joke.

And that we are DOOMED to be the playthings of chaos.

Choosing to Be Rude

Or

Nothing Lasts

Years ago, my friend Kathryn conducted a research study exploring what happened when the Canadian government began inviting "survivors" to participate in mental health policy development. It was a ground-breaking idea, intending that the people most affected might for the first time have a meaningful voice in how mental health services got shaped. But when survivors began to get involved in meetings there was trouble.

Kathryn's interviews with government workers and health professionals surfaced numerous complaints about survivors' participation. Interviewees described them as too loud, too personal, too often using unsavoury language, too prone to interrupting, too argumentative and too impolite. In short, they were rude. Rude because they were interrupting the implicit agreements that allowed discourse to proceed in its usual manner. People were very upset about these violations. It disturbed their comfort.

Sidebar: A more recent study in the U.S. also studied the ways in which mental health survivors participated in policy development forums. The researchers did not find the same problems as in Kathryn's study. It turned out that because rudeness was such a cultural norm nobody noticed that there were crazy people in the room.

I tell this story about rudeness now, because it's on my mind. I'm going to have to be rude. I can't abide by our implicit agreements. I hope you'll forgive me.

So, having given fair warning, I want to remind you that you can't hold on to anything and that you're going to die. Sorry. I just couldn't beat around the bush any longer. I know my words have an impact. I saw your body jerk back from the screen when you read them. And the look on your face was exactly what I've come to expect. You know, something like, "I bloody well know that things don't last and I don't need you to remind me and I don't like to be reminded and fuck right off."

It's ok. That happens all the time when I bring up impermanence.

It's really quite remarkable, that a feature that is so much a part of everyday reality remains so hidden and so unpopular. It's as if we constantly seek an illusion of permanence and when something pierces the bubble of our illusion, we don't like it.

> Sidebar: There is a social psychology theory about illusion being a foundation of good mental health, which draws on findings that show that people who underestimate the likelihood of bad things happening (e.g. dying on the way to work today) have a stronger sense of well being than people who accurately estimate the likelihood of being hit

by a bus. Which seems to lead to a conclusion that to be mentally healthy and thus normal is to be bat shit crazy.

Let me turn again to research to further illuminate our attitudes towards impermanence, and refer to a study about what happens for people who have a colleague die. Across multiple offices where deaths occurred, researchers found that 70% of people ignored the death entirely, or limited their response to no more than two, "Isn't that terrible" statements. Another 20% sent an email or card of condolence to the family of the deceased, and then put it out of their mind. Of the 10% who thought about attending the funeral, one-third actually did. From among that group, exactly half fantasized about their next summer vacation during the eulogy. Of those who actually allowed themselves to be temporarily pierced by the truth of impermanence, a majority reported waves of irrational anger and then drank heavily after the funeral so that they could forget. A smaller group became actively worried about their own eventual death and sought prescriptions for anxiety from their doctors. A final few were very sad about the loss of their colleague and the reality of impermanence.

That's pretty compelling research evidence in support of my contention that people react poorly to impermanence. Which is why I fabricated it to support my argument. But that's how it is these day with researchers, having finally learned at the feet of politicians. We can just make things up and if it's compelling and supports our world view then we've done our job and done it well.

And in a situation like mine, where the false news helps reveal a real news story, it all comes out in the wash.

Ok, I can feel I've lost a few of you with all this heavy data talk. Let me be more prosaic.

It's like we all went on a picnic to the park down at the foot of the Scarborough bluffs, and ate our old cheese and dill pickle sandwiches, and basked in the sun. But we were absolutely careful to never rudely mention the possibility that this moment might end and that the night would come. You know, as if by not talking about the night we could avoid acknowledging that it exists and could continue to slather on more sunscreen, eating sandwiches until we get seriously bloated. But we actually wouldn't even consider the possibility of eventual indigestion, because we just wouldn't want our sunlit bubble to burst. And if anyone at the picnic rudely blurted out that they hoped they would get a good sleep tonight the rest of us would look at them sideways, and feel a slight dip in the collective mood, and quickly ask for some beer to go with the sandwiches.

> Sidebar: I know that drinking beer in a public park remains illegal in Toronto, but it was a compelling idea so I included it as if we would in truth actually break the law to help us avoid thinking of the dark night to come.

I hope it's clear by now. We really, really don't like impermanence.

Which brings me back to DOOM, and to how all of our efforts to avoid sinking into its welcoming arms cause us so much grief. Really, what's so terrible about impermanence?

Oh boy, I may have to close down my non-existent twitter account if I get more reactions like that. I really don't need that kind of input. It hurts my feelings.

Maybe I was minimizing it a bit, suggesting that impermanence isn't terrible. I get that it is terrible in some ways. Like when my favourite serving bowl, that I bought on a sunny afternoon in the park when I was a young man and felt on top of the world, finally cracked and broke the other day. It pained me to feel that loss. Truly. But I also felt intimately connected to that beautiful bowl in its passing. Paradoxically, being pierced by that moment of impermanence made me feel really alive.

I own a mala, which is a string of beads around my wrist. Mine is made up of carved bone in the shape of human skulls. Fingering the skulls reminds me of impermanence, and that's like a staccato influx of energy, hit after hit of everything coming apart.

Last year, in a fit of generosity I gave skull malas to all my friends and family for Christmas. If I'm to be truly honest, it was not my most successful gift-giving experiment. On the upside, people made quite a lot of room for me at the dinner table and for once I got my fair share of the festive feast. On the downside, two months later on my birthday I was given three Metallica t-shirts, a playlist of old Twisted Sister songs, and a gift certificate to the local piercing boutique. Also on the downside, my sister has taken to sending me weekly texts to remind me that she knows a good exorcist.

I didn't intend to upset them all so much, just like I don't intend to upset you. But, perhaps naively, I wanted to let people in on the open secret. Namely that hanging out in the constant change of impermanence is just way better than attempting to avoid it.

It's worth a try.

My Brilliant Analysis of the <u>Sons of Anarchy</u>

Or

Family as the Ultimate Conspiracy

We might both exhale deeply and give thanks that we're done with impermanence, at least as a topic in this book. And we probably should just enjoy some release and a moment of ease before we wade further into the darkness, into the very heart of DOOM. I'm talking, of course, about family.

Years ago, in the early days of my adventures in therapy, I was just getting going one session in describing some typical family tensions when my therapist interrupted, "Why do you have anything to do with those people?" That stopped me dead (that's a figure of speech, I'm really not trying to slip in more impermanence messaging). While I certainly agreed that my family had problems, I hadn't ever thought of it as SO terrible that I should cut all ties to protect myself. But I misunderstood. She was saying that as an adult, having no children at that point, I had a choice about who I hung out with and how much. That I need not feel obliged to family. That was a radical thought, and it began my long and dangerous investigation into probably the biggest conspiracy of all time.

Just to be on the safe side, I'd rather you didn't share this part of my manuscript with your parents. Or siblings. Or cousins.

A pivotal turning point in my investigation occurred in that hopeful stretch where I was actually using the elliptical machine, working out and simultaneously watching all seven seasons of *The Sons of Anarchy*. If any of you missed this important docudrama, it features a motorcycle gang involved in crime. While the story was rich with intrigue, treachery and violence, it was the commentary on family that kept me coming back.

There can be no doubt that Jacks and the other Sons and the women who loved them were contributing to the fabric of society. Drugs, sex and gambling are all clearly necessary for our collective survival. And in that way the club was just like families, which are also engaged in important actions, supporting the development of children into adults who have more skills than knowing how to play Fortnite, order pizza, and let someone else do all the laundry. So, let's be clear, I am not suggesting we should do away with either crime or families.

In my rich fantasy life, I conducted a survey with the Sons of Anarchy and asked them what they valued the most in their lives. The answers were evenly mixed between living freely and riding their bikes, with a lot of conflation between the two responses. But anyone who studied the show would easily suss out that they were just being shy about what was really most important. Which was the sense of belonging that came with being a loyal member of the club. Caring for each other, committed to scheming and killing with their brothers and sisters. Like some kind of super-family for the violently inclined.

As the seasons progressed, and the writing got worse, the central tension continued to build. While claiming they wanted to be free, the characters made one absolutely idiotic decision after another in order not to let the gang down. Which locked them yet more tightly within the dysfunctional prison of their familial intimacy. For example (spoiler alert!), they decided to start trafficking guns in a big way even though they didn't want to, but in order to ensure the stability and survival of the gang. It drove me crazy. Please, if you're going to be a gun runner, do it because it's a calling, not because you feel like you must preserve the gang at all costs, or out of misplaced guilt for not loving your gang well enough.

So, yes, gangs and families are important, but they are both trying to take over the world. Worse than Amazon, Google and Facebook. Watch out! What started out as a commitment to freedom and independence has morphed into an evil tyranny that attempts to rule our loyalties, decisions, and statutory holidays.

I hope I'm not understating things. People sometimes say I should be more forthright.

How could families have come to be such a strong influence in our lives? It has to do with informed consent, or the absence thereof. Let me explain.

When a baby is born, she is not typically given the opportunity to sign an informed consent form. I'm not exactly sure why that is, but maybe in part because she's not yet able to hold a pen. So, she's pretty much stuck with whatever she gets. In contrast, her parents have consented, implicitly or explicitly, to shoulder the job of taking care of this baby. And they get all the power to define how that will look.

Hmmm! You've got to wonder about this. And you've also got to wonder why no lawyers are involved. That's really suspicious, because it's not like lawyers are in the habit of overlooking potential income streams. Who's looking out for the baby's best interests?

"The parents", you say. Silly me, why didn't I think of that. But seriously, let's just imagine that in a reasonably equitable world there would be a child advocate for every baby. Said advocate would want to ensure on behalf of the baby that conditions of living in the family would support the major reason for having a family, i.e., that she would be supported to grow up to be an independent, fully functioning member of society. And that any expectations for the baby, and later child, and even later teenager, would have to be entirely consistent with that mandate.

While that is a common-sense rationale, the advocate seasoned in family treachery would likely deem it necessary to spell out what wouldn't be allowable. And introduce riders like:

- Parent instructions to the child must be reasonable and defensible, and can not revert to, "Because I told you so."
- Career guidance cannot be limited to doctor, lawyer, engineer, or literary agent.

- Hygiene requirements should not have to exceed those commonly found in the IT departments at Amazon, Google and Facebook.
- Stories about the parent's own childhood should never be told, no matter how fascinating, unless they have clear application to the child's eventual survival in a world the parents are poorly prepared to inhabit.

It's all well and good to spin this type of fantasy about how things would be if equity mattered. But at least we can be reassured that children eventually reach the Age of Consent, and are then able to choose freely. Can't we?

Of course.

As I'm sure happened for you, on the day after I reached legal age, we had a big family meeting. We were all a bit hungover, so we took our time getting down to business. There was a celebratory mood in the air, natural because we were all happy that I was now a certifiable adult and free to make my own choices. Everyone agreed that all former deals were off, and that any new arrangements with the family were entirely negotiable. There would be no assumed expectations for matters like: attendance at Thanksgiving; whether or how often I would make contact with family members; whether I would choose to listen to advice about career paths, such as joining a motorcycle gang; whether, if I had children at some future time, they would need to spend time with their grandparents; whether I would give any thought at all about how to care for my parents when they got even older than they already were, including how to get them to leave their rundown bungalow when it's all collapsing around them and they're too frail to manage but refuse to listen to reason. It was all up for grabs!

Oh, that didn't happen for you? Or you? Or you? Or you? Which would suggest that free will is just so much malarkey when it comes to family.

Wait, you say, you do exercise choice that goes against the expectations, like when you traveled to Crete and missed Thanksgiving in 2007. Or when you chose to take the kids to summer camp instead of spending a "restful" week at Grandma's.

Fair enough. But did you feel guilty? That's the real kicker in this conspiracy of family. That no matter how terrible, or dysfunctional the family, not abiding by the long list of expectations results in life-threatening attacks of guilt. And for most of us there is a low hum of guilt in the background all the time. You know, like, "your mom would like to hear from you."

There's something you need to know that will help. Right under your left shoulder blade, if you can twist your arm to reach back there, is an almost imperceptible rise in the skin. If you are more flexible than I am in my old age you'll eventually find it. That's where they put the microchip. Right after they cut the umbilical cord.

This is not some kind of weird conspiracy stuff. It was posted on the Internet by very credible occultists. But it's so helpful to know that it's not just that you are weak-willed or entirely neurotic (although that can also be true), it's that you have been programmed from birth to feel really bad whenever you are not aligned with the family conspiracy directive, to always put family first.

Even though you are DOOMED to be oppressed by all the pressures of family, you still get to choose what you do. And you can also feel what you feel and still survive, able to Gallivant through it all. And here's a secret. It's possible to sing, *What Do You Do With a Drunken Sailor* at the top of your voice and feel guilt at the same time.

Enough said.

Why Thanksgiving Should be Cancelled

Or

Why Family Ruins You For a Free Life

The fact that you're reading this book tells me a lot about you. That you're highly discriminating in your tastes, a deep thinker, and that you are always working to improve yourself. You're the kind of person who may have spent years in therapy or astrological study to explore yourself. You are also likely to have worked hard to learn to stretch and breathe and eat mindfully, centring yourself and enhancing well being at every turn. And you push your body, maybe running or squash or water polo, so that you release stress and avoid meltdowns most of the time.

All that effort to improve! And then it's time for the family Thanksgiving dinner. Oh boy, talk about coming down to earth. It can be discouraging.

I used to say that Thanksgiving was my favorite holiday, mostly because it was about being grateful and, yes, I have a lot to be grateful for. I thought of it as a less loaded holiday, freed from the religious overlay and consumerist nonsense of some of the other holidays. But somewhere along the way I realized that it wasn't so benign and, indeed, that there was a major program of indoctrination being enacted. Namely, that what we most need to be grateful for is family, and showing up for Thanksgiving dinner is proof that we are in compliance with the prime directive.

Why are family get-togethers so challenging?

When I was in training to become a psychologist, I did an internship at a government agency called Child and Youth Services, it's mandate being to help kids with mental health issues. The zeitgeist of the time was dominated by something called family systems theory, which emphasized that you couldn't understand a child's problems without understanding the family. So, to help a child meant intervening with the family.

Sidebar: Family systems therapy is much less in vogue these days, as more and more kids caught on to the idea that they could make a lot of trouble and, strictly speaking, it wouldn't be their fault. Like if a 10-year-old boy burned the house down in a fit of rage, the therapists would soon enough be talking with the parents about how their rage with each other, expressed through constant arguing, was being expressed through the boy. And they would have the parents doing exercises to communicate better while the boy was sneaking off to the washroom to set fires.

Why is family systems therapy relevant here? Because it points at something true. Which is that kids are motivated to find a way to survive in their families, and they take on ways of behaving that are likely to meet that goal. You know, whatever it takes.

The real problem is not that kids do what they need to do in order to survive. That's actually very smart of them. It's adaptive for their situation. Of course, you should hide under the bed to avoid dad when he's drinking and violent, which is most of the time. The problem is generalization, which is the natural assumption that if it worked in the family, it will work everywhere. And, besides, it's all you know how to do. Like when twenty years later you get stuck under the bed when the neighbour drops by to ask to borrow your ladder. Or you refuse to turn your camera on in your Zoom meeting with the boss. It turns out that hiding is not always adaptive.

So somewhere along the way you realize that your usual way of being in the world doesn't work all the time. And you decide to change. To open yourself up to other possibilities. You take a course in public speaking, and then give a speech on the moral benefits of hockey, deliberately letting yourself be seen and heard. It's a good first step, although the brawl afterwards leads to a brief setback. For the first time since the marriage, you stand up to your spouse and she ends up taking the garbage out herself. After the divorce, you post your picture on the dating app and boldly state your bedroom preferences. It's all exhilarating, to feel that you can survive life without having to hide all the time. And, of course, you take up therapy, yoga, and running.

But, then, inevitably Thanksgiving rolls around again. It seems like it should be just fine, because you have all this hard-won confidence and a bunch of super new coping skills. And, besides, dad is now really old and couldn't beat you up if he tried and he's been going to AA meetings for a decade. And mom is mostly deaf, and so doesn't get outraged by dad's racist, sexist, and anti-vegan statements, and no longer provokes him into a rage. And yet, five minutes in the door and you've stopped talking, gone to the bathroom 7 times, and are desperately trying to manage your longing for the underside of the bed.

That's just how it is. Family ruins you for a free life. And the moment you start to get the tiniest taste of more freedom, it snaps you back. It's hopeless. You're DOOMED.

But you have to admit, if the bed isn't too low to the ground, it can be quite wonderful to just lie underneath and listen to your heart beat. And dinners only last so long, and it's just a swamp that can be sloshed through on the path back to higher ground.

It's all good.

Although if there were a vote, mine would be to cancel Thanksgiving.

Selling Water by the Bank of a River

Or

Capitalism Rules Us All

Writers should always ground their work in theory. Keeping that in mind, I went looking this morning for a seminal reference book for today's topic. But *The Protestant Ethic and the Spirit of Capitalism* by Max Weber was nowhere to be found. That's really too bad, because it lays out one possible reason for why capitalism bloomed in the 17th century, namely that a particular strain of Protestantism that was popular at the time, and which had some expression in the Baptist tradition I grew up in, emphasized that profit and success were signs of God's favour. As you well know, capitalism is all about profit and so there was a natural co-arising of the two streams, such that to get rich also meant that you were likely on your way to heaven. Of course, after things got rolling, Capitalism quickly ditched religion because it hemmed things in on the morality front, making it difficult for entrepreneurs like the Sons of Anarchy to make a decent go of things.

But, alas, the book was gone. We'd gotten rid of it, or as we like to say in our home, we "Marie Kondo'd" it. You do know about Marie Kondo, I hope. Author of *The Life-Changing Magic of Tidying Up*, and host of a Netflix show where she tiptoes into homes and helps people tidy, organize and most of all reduce. She suggests that you make your decisions about what to keep and what to get rid of on the basis of joy (although if you really need something, like say a garlic press, it's ok to keep it even if it's not joy-making). This approach to reducing definitely has a stronger appeal than others that encourage you to prepare to die by first tidying things up. Impermanence is definitely a poor marketing gambit.

There are reasons to be skeptical of the Marie Kondo gig. For one, it assumes a kind of socioeconomic privilege, that you have enough space and income to have accumulated excessive goods, and that you can afford to get rid of anything. So that puts me in the frame once again. I am, indeed, privileged to have accumulated more than I strictly need. And just to remind you, I am also indefensibly old, white, and male. Another problem with Marie's scheme is that it can create tensions in households where joy does not arise the same for everyone. Like when I decided that I would keep all my t-shirts and sweatpants because they give me joy. To my surprise, those same objects do not give Kerry any joy at all ("it's not you who has to look at them!").

As you've gathered, Kerry and I decided to take the Marie Kondo trip, which meant weeks of sorting through all the objects in our home, while Benten looked at us sideways from her perch in front of the gaming console. Crazy parents! And while for the most part we liked the ride, with its consequent wide-open spaces in drawers and closets and photo albums, we really did get rid of a whole bunch of things that we'd like back. Like the Max Weber book.

Poor Marie Kondo has created some heavy karma for herself.

This isn't just some wild tangent. It ties back to Capitalism, because Marie Kondo, she of the anti-capitalist notion of reducing unnecessary goods and consumption, turns out to be a consummate capitalist.

Right after we finished with the trips to the dump, and to Charity Village, and to my sister (bearing gifts is a nifty strategy to draw attention away from the possibility of being demon-possessed), we found out that Marie has an online store. Where she sells, wait for it … all kinds of useless trinkets. Like a tuning fork and clear quartz crystal to promote inner balance, (just $75). Like a ceramic spice jar with bamboo lid. Like a woven rattan desktop organizer.

I was shocked. Maybe she really thinks these things are cool, but I'll bet that if she looks to see if they evoke joy two months from now, she'll feel as nauseous as I do. And, here's a terrible paranoid thought. I wonder if she's been visiting Charity Village to buy the cast-offs from people who've followed her program and, now she's selling them in her online store. Nasty thoughts. Doesn't mean they're not true.

Capitalism is rooted in a notion of continuous economic growth, which means finding more and more things to sell to more and more markets. At the time I was first reading Max Weber I was deep into a fling with Karl Marx, who was quite eloquent about all the ways that Capitalism inevitably causes suffering for all those except the biggest Whos. I eventually discovered that Karl also had his blind spots but, ultimately, it doesn't really matter what Karl or you or I think of Capitalism because it has totally won. Its voracious appetite swallows us all. Even Marie Kondo.

As a second-year university student I was convinced that Capitalism would soon implode because there were only so many markets and only so many things that people would want or need. Boy was I wrong. Capitalism is like the COVID-19 virus, just keeps morphing into new and more dangerous expressions, holding us all ransom to its relentless growth.

Capitalism is also very wily, gets us to want things that no sane person wants, and turns everything into commodities for purchase. Even things that don't even exist. Just ask the Bitcoin sales people. What's at the bottom of that great big Ponzi scheme? Is there anything you can touch or eat or smell?

Which brings us to the spiritual marketplace.

At the funeral in 1961 of one of the great Zen masters of modern time, Sogaku Harada, there hung a piece of calligraphy written by him. It read:

For forty years I've been selling water

By the bank of a river.

Ho, ho!

My labors have been wholly without merit.

This remarkable teacher, who lived in a spartan monastery on the harsh coast of the Japan Sea, was making a joke. About the ridiculous futility of trying to transfer to other people something (we could call it the Nature of Mind, or any of a hundred other names) that exists everywhere, all the time, as if it were special and somehow separate from our own nature. Yet, that's what he did, point a generation of spiritual seekers at what was right in front of their eyes. All that they would need would be to learn to pay attention. Contrary to the tongue-in-cheek implications of the calligraphy, profit was in no way part of the equation.

And then there's mindfulness. Which can be defined as the awareness that arises from paying attention, on purpose, in the present moment. Which sounds an awful lot like what Sogaku Harada was "selling" by his river. Something free and totally accessible to those who are able to attend.

Just now I Googled "executive mindfulness". The first website I opened included this information: "Join us for the extraordinary chance to study Mindful Leadership with world-class teachers while living in luxury and enjoying organic meals by a private chef." Like other really elite programs, there is no mention of money. Clearly, it's assumed that you're loaded and don't need to concern yourself with the trivial. My spidey senses are suddenly alert to profiteering. To Capitalism writ large.

Benten, my dear no-bullshit daughter, did a paper on mindfulness for her religious studies class. In it, she argued that mindfulness has been coopted by neo-liberal Capitalist forces as a way to make people more willing and able to put up with toxic, inequitable workplaces. You know, keep them down where they belong by helping them cope better. And it can also help executives to rule more effectively. I quote again from the website I referred to above, "Mindful leadership is the next competitive advantage." Ho, ho.

Is mindfulness training just a mug's game? Even granted Benten's critique, I think not. People benefit from being able to simply pay attention. But has it been coopted by Amazon, Google and Facebook? Definitely.

So, once again, we're DOOMED. Commodification has become as ubiquitous as breathing. We can only watch how it keeps happening and make our decisions about how much to be swept along by the mighty pull of the river.

Which brings me to the store under development on my website. Pricing will be competitively outrageous. My site includes products that will be familiar to today's shoppers, such as t-shirts, sweatshirts, baseball caps, and towels, in a variety of colors and embroidered with pithy sayings, like:

- I am Nobody Important too.
- I'm with Nobody Important (for the codependent couples out there)
- Let's Go Gallivanting
- Happy DOOM to you

I will also be offering written satirical pieces by commission. My specialties are toasts to the DOOMED couple, and speeches to celebrate family values at Thanksgiving. Price will be negotiated according to the potential danger for me, where the more lethal the wit the more it will cost you.

Finally, I will take Capitalism to new heights, by offering a product of no worth whatsoever at the highest price I can get away with. It's brilliant. I will sell you Nothing, in 2" x 2" boxes, 6 per order. Shipping is not strictly necessary, but I'll charge for it anyway.

Check out my website (www.nobodyimportant.ca).

The Power of Yodeling

Or

A Collaborative Study of Anxiety

Like all good writers, I always prepare the way for a forthcoming discussion by signalling what I will be talking about. I don't want to surprise you, do I?

Here we go. This is about anxiety, what it is, what causes it, why it's a problem, and what we can do about it. Very good organizational structure to this discussion. Lowers anxiety because there will be less uncertainty for you as things unfold.

Further to that lowering uncertainty intention, I would like to reassure you that this chapter will not mention the Sons of Anarchy, death and impermanence, old cheese and dill pickle sandwiches, or the Ten Commandments.

Also, so you feel in safe hands, which should lower your anxiety, let me remind you that I am a psychologist. I know a lot about mental health, and because I am a serious and responsible professional you can relax in the knowledge that I'd never bullshit you. Especially not about anything as tender as the anxiety that you feel when you're being reminded about how anxious you are.

As you know, anxiety is being flagged every day in the media as a growing problem, especially among youth. So, because I'm old and totally out of touch with the particular flavor of anxiety among young ones I've recruited an expert consultant. My daughter Benten is a student of anxiety, knows a lot about it from all that time hiding under the sheets, and is really pissed off that it causes so much trouble for her and her friends. So, dear readers, please welcome Benten to this learned discussion.

We will start at the beginning, which is all very predictable and reassuring.

Ok. I've had some feedback that might change how this goes. Benten didn't actually say this out loud. She's of the opinion that human beings should preserve their energy as much as possible and thus not make unnecessary exertions. Like talking. Fortunately, I've gotten very good at reading the muscle twitches at the corners of her mouth. Which is how I know that she is not keen at all on my proposed structure for approaching our topic. And a bit irritated about my "acting like a psychologist again, trying to define and control everything!"

"Who cares how you define anxiety. Like, duh, people can figure that out themselves."

"And who cares why it happens. It happens! Why don't you just go to the important part, which is what people can do about it."

"And no, before you ask, I do not want to empty the dishwasher."

I like collaborative projects. I really do.

The trick with collaboration is to thank people for their input and then do what you want. I wonder if that's an original thought?

So let me provide a succinct definition of anxiety.

Anxiety is fear's kissing cousin. Less dramatic, less screaming or running out of the room, but often more insidious and pervasive. Like, I feel threatened but I'm not entirely sure why, or there may be a bunch of reasons but I can't begin to list them all. Like maybe an alien spaceship will land in the backyard, maybe Tony Robbins will sue me for slander, maybe the government will find out I'm not charging sales tax on my boxes of nothing, maybe the neighbours have judgements about my sweatpants, maybe I'm not a good enough writer and not the least bit funny. And so on. Endless worries, many not even fully articulated to myself, all waiting in the wings to surprise and terrorize me. And I should be prepared to deal with each and every possible catastrophe, effectively and bravely. Will I be prepared!? And knowing from my track record that I'm really bad at dealing with difficult things that come at me. Sometimes, I just freeze like a bunny about to be devoured by a monk turned fox. And it makes me wonder why I'm not better at life, who I really am, and how it could all have gone so terribly wrong.

So that's anxiety. Why is it a problem? Because it feels uncomfortable. And, more importantly, because it keeps people from doing things that they should do and sometimes want to do.

Ok, ok. I _am_ getting on with it.

Benten and I have done our Google research thoroughly and we've identified the top recommended strategies for managing anxiety. We'll proceed in an orderly fashion, taking them one at a time, with Benten's expert opinion offered after each heading.

- Connect with Other People: It can be good to talk with people, but not always. You probably don't want me to tell you every time I'm anxious about whether I locked my locker, even though there's nothing in my locker. It really, really annoys me to have thoughts like that, but it's my life so it's a little bit interesting to me but clearly not to you. And, also, talking to you about being afraid of dying will not reassure me.

- Exercise: Walks are nice, but I'm not sure they reduce anxiety. I crossed the road to avoid people even before COVID.

- Get a Good Sleep: Of course, you should sleep. But it's not like, "Oh, great, I slept for 16 hours and now I have no fears!"

- Take a Break from Screens: I've never tried it. A lot of people say it's helpful.

- Meditate: It's boring, and so all you can do is think. And that makes you more anxious.

- Identify and Challenge Negative Thoughts: It helps a bit, but I still doubt myself. If I trusted myself, I'd know I was crazy and wouldn't believe all this irrational stuff.

- Use Positive Self Talk: I like the idea. Fake it till you make it. But it's hard to take it seriously when I switch from "this art is so bad I should trash it" to "this is the Mona Lisa".

- Limit Social Media Contact: I know that people compare themselves all the time with other people on social media. But it's not like pre-technology people like you didn't make comparisons by reading magazines or watching black and white films.

- Be Helpful and Volunteer: Whenever you see ads about people making a difference about social justice or climate change it's always like, "youth are our future". Thanks a lot! You think that makes me feel calm?

- Ease Up On That Achievement Drive: Lots of kids think they have to study all the time, and get the best marks and end up at the best universities. At least I'm not like that. A good thing with the online schooling in the pandemic is that it's easier to cheat and that probably takes some pressure off.

This is where I sweep in and nicely summarize.

It seems that there are a lot of different strategies that might help reduce anxiety to some degree under some conditions. But at the end of the day, the likelihood appears to be strong that anxiety will still be an issue.

By now, you should know how this will go.

We are DOOMED!

It's comforting that in this chaotic and unpredictable world we keep coming back to this same central truth.

To be DOOMED about anxiety is to know that we will always experience anxiety, coming and going, more and less, in our lives.

How, you may ask, can DOOM work it's healing powers with anxiety. Firstly, we can get friendly with the experience, learn to lean into the jitters and the nausea and talk nice to the waves of heat and racing thoughts. Surely, it's just a preference that we imagine the feeling of, for example, love to be better than anxiety. In an equitable world, anxiety would be recognized and validated for its particular contributions to human experience. We could cultivate a new kind of relationship and redress generations of emotive oppression.

DOOM also heals by exploding the fruitless pursuit of hope that we will one day be cool dudes (or whatever they call those kinds of people these days), and forces us to do the hard, awkward work of acting despite the discomfort and potential humiliation. You know, I may be uncomfortable about going out the front door but if I don't want to wait until my parents kick me out or I rot in the basement I guess I better JUST DO IT.

So that's the bottom line with anxiety. To act anyway. As Benten says, it's what you do when you don't have any other choice.

Not exactly a Gallivanting vibe is it. But wait. There are ways to help move that JUST DO IT agenda forward more actively, with a bit more joie de vivre. A fancy term for it is "exposure treatment", which simply means embodying your own worst nightmare. I am particularly skilled at suggesting specific applications. Like:

- Yodel for your online classmates
- Stand on the street corner wearing a placard that says, "I hide under the blankets"
- Explain to the waiter that you have a urinary infection and need to drink lots of water.
- Tell everyone on the bus, one at a time, that you are extremely happy to meet them.

Needless to say, really anxious people are less likely to go for exposure treatment than for medication (or cannabis or alcohol). But, crazily enough, those willing to walk into the fire, and who live to tell the tale, report the greatest reductions in ongoing anxiety.

Go figure.

As I always say, DOOM pays.

Hockey as a Somewhat Successful Coping Strategy

Or

The Case for Climbing Mount DOOM

The eye of Mordor turns in a slow circle and takes in the state of the world. It's not a pretty sight.

The Beatles captured the sentiment. "I read the news today, oh boy".

We're in pandemic lockdown today here in Toronto, which we've been in and out of for a long time. Pretty much everyone I've talked to is some version of stark raving mad.

And, of course, the COVID plague merely sits on top of everything else that we don't want to know or have to deal with.

Icebergs melting, storming the Capitol, sex trafficking, extinction, George Floyd, forests burning, coral reefs dying, normalizing paedophilia, opioid deaths, hormone-infused meat, drug company conspiracies, poisoned drinking water, depleting ozone layer, rolling pandemics, homelessness, environmental illnesses, everyday genocide, rising suicide rates, rioting in the streets.

In the *Lord of the Rings*, Frodo the hobbit is charged with the formidable task of travelling into the heart of a great darkness. He carries with him a ring, that must be destroyed, for there to be any viable future. To destroy the ring, he must climb Mount

DOOM and throw it into the molten fires. The closer Frodo gets to the top, the more he is weighed down by his task, the greater his desire to collapse and just give over to the forces of evil.

This is not at all like our current situation. For one thing, I have a skin sensitivity and couldn't wear a ring made by an evil sorcerer. For another, DOOM is given an altogether one-sided and unfair depiction in Frodo's story. Could it be that the evil assigned to those sorcerers and goblins are merely post-hoc interpretations that have been fabricated by the eventual winners of the war, those nasty hobbits and humans and elves and dwarves?

But, still, the story has some resonance. This challenge of Gallivanting through the DOOM is not easy. The mountain is steep. And, like Frodo, I feel the weight of it all, the sometimes longing to just lie down in an indentation in the rock and drift off to sleep.

What is clearly called for is a direct and lively exploration of the further possibilities for Gallivanting, and a more fulsome consideration of what makes it possible to cohabitate happily with DOOM.

We'll get to that. But first we need to take a detour, to take a careful look at the main coping strategies that we humans commonly use to avoid climbing Mount DOOM. You know, climb the little hill just to the left because it's easier. Or, take a year or more off to travel before deciding whether Mount DOOM is a priority. Or, head home to the Shire where we can once again focus on nothing more pressing than our second breakfast each morning.

Here we go.

<u>Focus on Really Stupid, Irrelevant Things</u>: This may be the primary coping mechanism of our times. It has its advantages. Let me demonstrate.

Tonight, the Toronto Maple Leafs are playing the Montreal Canadians. It's a nothing hockey game as far as the standings go, but it's the last week of the regular season and then playoffs begin. So, you can feel the intensity building, and these two teams will meet in the first round and they want to send a message to each other about how that series will go. You know, start the intimidation now. Did you know that the Leafs have not won the Stanley Cup since 1967 and that they have the best shot at it this year because they have talented young stars like Austin Mathews, who can use his stick like nobody I've ever seen, together with tough veterans like Mike Foligno. The goaltending will be a big question. Will Campbell continue to be able to play above his level? Will Anderson …

Do you now how long I could go on with this kind of drivel? I probably lost half my readership with just that one paragraph. Kerry would have gotten up and left the room before I finished the first sentence.

But it's a kind of coping, and it kind of works. While I was thinking about the game tonight, I felt no pain at all. Except when I remembered all the other series the Leafs lost when I had that same thought "this might be the year" …

It could be worse. I could have gone on about how each of the Kardashians may be feeling about their show ending.

Now my intention here is not to suggest that you or I should avoid stupid, irrelevant thoughts and activities. Not at all. I stand by my right to watch lots of hockey. But can it be a problem? You bet. For one thing, it can really torpedo harmony in family relations. Benten goes into a twitching frenzy every time I even say the word hockey. For another, it's easy to get lost in a fantasy universe that bears no resemblance to how things actually are.

Let's just say that the Leafs win this year. I know, I know. But it could happen. I will feel happy for a couple of days. Then a little depressed when I realize that it doesn't actually affect my life. That Bruins fans will not just all spontaneously come to realize that they're losers and that we're winners and apologize for their longstanding arrogance. That I'll still have to take the garbage out tomorrow, that there will be another vote to see who will get to vote next time around, that a new variant will infest the news, that I will not be getting a million-dollar bonus because the Leafs won, despite having invested my goodwill and energy all these years cheering them on.

My dissatisfaction will return, like it always does. And I'll have no way to tolerate it so will have to start watching lots of baseball, which is ever so less satisfying.

Focus on Less Stupid, Less Irrelevant Things: The pandemic has really put a spotlight on this type of coping. Knitting sweaters. Building wooden cabinets. Taking an online photography course. In our household a winner early in the pandemic was baking sourdough bread. Kerry connived to get some starter from a neighbour, (not the professor), and later bought some more starter online to compare the differences. And then there was the drama of feeding and storing the starter, the eventual mixing, and rising, and kneading. Experiments with different shapes, different flours, adding molasses or coffee or cheese or raisins or seeds. Worlds within worlds to explore.

Apart from the weight gain, it was all quite wonderful. And it helped to cope with the pandemic and everything else. More recently, the focus has shifted to gardening but I'm not allowed to write about that because I'm told (in a very authoritarian tone of voice) that there is nothing the least bit stupid or irrelevant about gardening, which is a pure path to make the world a better place. I find that it's sometimes in my best interest to accept things that I'm told without so much as a twitch.

So, it's hard to be critical of hobbies as a coping strategy. And yet, passions can drift into obsessions, and whole armies of bakers and knitters (maybe even gardeners?) have gone missing from action, chasing their version of delight, and abandoning the rest of us who have to wake up each day and deal with the truth that the world is on fire.

Focus on Forming Opinions: A tried and tested way of coping with difficult, uncertain times is to become certain about things. We become certain by deciding that we know how things are, what's right and what's wrong, and who's great and who should be punished.

Sometimes you meet people that are really sophisticated about opinions. They probably grew up in homes where the family sat around the dinner table and debated the issues of the day. Their idea of a good time is to have it out at length about taxation philosophies, immigration policy, models of education, and the rights of the fetus.

Dinner wasn't like that in my household. Opinions were not there to be thoughtfully debated, merely asserted. Like, "that's a dumb idea", or "they're all just lazy".

Sophisticated or not, opinions make people feel secure and safe. And having them shows that you're smart, even when it's so obviously not the case. Of course, the internet has been very useful in democratizing the expression of opinions. Which is only fair. Why should only the smart people get to cope by being arrogantly self-righteous in public forums?

Is there a downside to being opiniated? Let me count the downsides. The big one is that it's impossible to have an open mind when you already know the answer. Which makes it hard to be creative in approaching anything, including all the problems of our time.

To allow DOOM in would be to admit that mostly we don't know. Not a clue! And to be willing to look at all the possibilities each time to see what, if anything, makes sense. You know, back in the day it made sense that people not be expected to wear masks. That would have been total totalitarian oppression. And kinky to boot. And yet today, I'm sure we all agree …

Focus on Fixing Things: It seems patently obvious that a good way of coping with difficult realities is to just fix them. Really, why would we need any other strategies?

Sometimes this works really well. Like if you're getting really annoyed listening to somebody complain, you just stop responding to their texts. Or you're hungry so you order take-out roti.

The problem comes with the assumption that every problem can be fixed. You know how that goes.

Like when you get diagnosed with cancer. Let's fix that.

Did you get a second opinion? Probably should cut out meat or dairy or wheat. Visualize bombarding the cancer cells. Think positive thoughts. Only do what you love. Do what the doctors say. Don't do what the doctors say. Get lots of exercise. But not too much. Trust in God.

Please do something to fix it so that we don't have to deal with this painful reality any more. JUST DO IT!

So, the chief problem with fixing as a coping strategy is that it doesn't always work. Sometimes nothing will fix it.

The other problem is that people who rely heavily on fixing to cope are immensely, and I mean really immensely, annoying, and put themselves in danger from people like me, with unresolved teenage authority issues. People who really hate being told what to do and may not always employ prosocial behaviour when responding to unwanted advice.

I think it's time to stop a moment and reflect.

Because I'm a sensitive sort, I'm becoming aware of a tsunami of rage headed my way. There seems to be some kind of shared indignance at my thesis that there is value in attending to DOOM. This is all a bit unnerving for me, but let me at least try to make my case clearer.

It's not actually that I'm suggesting that we fabricate or go looking for a pessimistic version of reality. There's no need to look, it's already here. Surrounding me in this room where I type. Surrounding you in that room where you read and fume. The point is that it takes a great deal of energy to ignore or refute the existence of the proverbial elephant in the room. I know that the

Canadian Conservative Party last month refused to accept that climate change exists. But really, there's only about a dozen people left in the country who'll take that seriously!? And how can they possibly sustain that delusion even a moment longer? These attempts to hide from DOOM diminish us. We get so small, so cut off from ourselves and our world.

Back when I was in high school, I was reading Kahlil Gibran by candlelight one night. In the book there is a wise teacher who is asked to, "tell us about joy and sorrow". The start of the teacher's response is, "Your joy is your sorrow unmasked.", the implication being that you can't get to joy without including sorrow. They need each other. It struck me when I read it. It still strikes me. So, hanging out with DOOM requires making room for it all, and that brings us in touch with everything, and we feel more alive. Instead of a forced and panicky kind of joy we get the real deal. And maybe we cry more. I keep a bucket beside the bed.

When we include DOOM it also connects us with action. Maybe we can't fix it all, but we can do something. And in doing something, we get to experience care. And in caring, we get to feel how much we love this world.

And how much we will miss it if it goes.

Give Your Cows a Large Meadow to Graze In

Or

Alien Invasion Is Our Best Hope

"Ya got trouble, my friend, right here

I say, trouble right here in River City"

Lyrics from The Music Man (1962)

It's true. I've got trouble. The house is in a turmoil, as Kerry and Benten are entirely unhappy with me. They want to know why I've gotten so serious? Why I've taken to wearing only my black t-shirts and sweatpants? And how it is that I seem to have blithely written off the future of the earth and everyone on it?

Especially when there are UFOs to give us all hope.

You can maybe see what I have to deal with here. It's not easy having to always be the stable one. You know, the voice of reason.

But I have to say, in this case they have a point. I shouldn't have overlooked UFOs.

Yesterday I read an article in the New Yorker about the Pentagon's growing interest in UFOs. The author describes a history of mostly flawed attempts over decades to study UFOs, burdened by a ferocious war between wacko believers and fascist debunkers. Through it all, there is enough evidence to suggest something is probably going on out there, and in just the last year the study of UFOs has been validated by the U.S. military. Since then, there's been an upsurge in reported sightings.

It seems then that Kerry and Benten may be absolutely right in their claim that our best hope for the survival of planet Earth is an alien invasion. What remains is to sort out the details.

Signage, for example. If we want them to know that we'd welcome making contact, sooner rather than later, and assuming they can't just read our minds, it would be good to have a marketing campaign. We want to be creative in our approach, bring in the best advertising minds to help. Clearly billboards won't be enough, and I'm not sure how social media advertising will translate into extraterrestrial markets. I was wondering if we might use the same contractors responsible for that wonderful wall in the southern U.S., and build a huge welcome mat. Maybe in Arizona. Or I'm sure the Canadian government would volunteer all of Saskatchewan. It's all just empty space out there anyway.

Now, making a welcome mat kind of assumes that we do really want those UFOs to land. And it's possible that we don't. If, for example, they have been scouting us as a possible food source, or because the enamel in our teeth is thought to be an aphrodisiac when ground into dust and snorted. But what's there to lose. At least this way somebody, somewhere, might have a really super orgasm.

Another possibility is that they're not exactly friendly, but they have a relatively benign agenda. Like, maybe they want to convert us to a new heathen religion? That might not be so bad, as long as blood sacrifices aren't involved. Maybe they want to enlist us in helping them make a new form of music, something even better than psychedelic rock. Or maybe they want us to labour in their mushroom farms. I can see that working. I like mushrooms and hanging out in dark places.

But maybe they don't have an agenda. It could be they are just friendly and want to be helpful. You know, helpful rulers.

I don't object, in principle, to the idea of being ruled by aliens. I mean, how much worse could it be?

One thing that would be critically important is to get off on the right foot with the aliens. Which means we'd want to have a superb spokesperson for all earthlings.

I've thought a lot about who might be the ideal advisor to the aliens and, no, you are not in the running. Without any false posturing, I'll come right out and say it. I nominate myself. After all, I'm tall and have a strong chin and look like a leader. And I'm a psychologist, which means I'll be able to quickly understand how the aliens tick and thus be able to control and manipulate them. And I'm charming, and occasionally funny, which will allow me to entertain and put them at ease. Most of all, I'm very able to provide sage advice on how best to rule humans.

I have to say that the idea of that kind of power, being chief advisor to the aliens, is a bit of a head trip. But I can be trusted to not abuse my responsibility. I would never be so petty as to use my power to enact long-denied justice. Go on sleeping soundly, Marie Kondo.

Hold on there, you say? Why would I assume that aliens want to rule us? Maybe they're really friendly, and just want to support us in being our best selves. You know, like in a democracy.

Before I respond, I'd just like to point out that I've demonstrated throughout this project a rather remarkable open-mindedness. It's just that I have my limits! I'll entertain any reasonable idea about anything, including the proper governing model for an alien infused culture. But I have no time to waste on pure poppycock, romantic storylines brought to us by Disney.

You see, democracy can only work when there is a respect for the process. And when elected people are capable of caring, even at the expense of votes. Seen many signs of that lately? Right. So, at the very least we would need a stretch of time spent rehabilitating humans before they would be able to responsibly handle power. You know, time when we can collectively remember what it's like to get along and to build bridges instead of bomb them. I think four generations might do the trick. Although when I consider those interesting folks who stormed the

Capitol Hill Building, together with all the people who are right now planning on bombing Toronto (including Saskatchewan farmers), I wonder if five generations might be better. It's really an empirical question as to how long, and under what conditions, zealots can be transformed into open-hearted cooperative types.

The ruler model I would like to recommend to the aliens is a little bit Tony Robbins, and a tad Brene Brown. It emphasizes being friendly and generous. I was thinking that I could use the analogy of cows in a meadow with them, where the idea is that you give your cows a really big open space to wander in. You make sure that there's plenty of food. Shelters to get out of the rain. Opportunities for creative growth, like cowpie art and cowbell ringing. Encouragement for initiative taken, like start-up dating apps or the development of new technologies (like more elegant milking machines). It would be great to paint murals, and make music to promote an easy-going vibe. Maybe play John Lennon in the elevators, "Imagine all the cows and people, living life in peace".

I'm sure that this kind of unconditional love, overseen by the aliens and their trusty advisor, would encounter little to no resistance. And difficult people, unlike you and I, would simply dissolve into the background or else transform. There would be nary a sign of ruthless profiteers, black market gun runners, holocaust deniers, literary agents, mansplainers, or vegans.

Right. You had the same reaction as I did when reflecting on that last paragraph, didn't you? So, I'm sure we both agree on a slight adjustment to the plan. We will definitely need an electric fence around the pasture. And some sticks to go with the carrots. A list of rules would be helpful. Here are a few to start the ball rolling:

- No guns
- No super rich, elite society cowshit
- No destroying the grass
- No abuse of animals
- No ornamental shrubs, only native species
- No selling useless, joyless things (you too Marie Kondo)
- No Thanksgiving dinners

Send me your ideas for more No's by email. I love to collaborate.

At some point down the line, if all goes well, we humans will be ready to take the reigns back from the aliens and make our long wished for utopia a reality. Although I have to say it makes me nervous to imagine the actual handover. It could be a bit like what is about to happen in Afghanistan, when the "peace keepers" leave. Chaos and carnage. Perhaps it would make more sense to have a transitional system for 10 or 20 years, where a human could be in charge but keep everything safe and under control. And who better than the chief advisor, a person well experienced with benevolent but firm rule. I'd be honoured to serve my planet…

And there you have it. Right back to DOOM. Even in the best-case alien invasion, we are in trouble.

Could it be otherwise?

A Taste of the Fruit Bowl Experience

Or

Going Beyond Difference

I get up early in the mornings, put the coffee on, and make bowls of fruit for our breakfast. This morning the fruit bowls included: apple, Asian pear, papaya, cantaloupe, mango, raspberries, and banana. Next time I go to the store I will be make new choices, renewing some fruits and replacing others according to what's available, how much it costs, what looks good, and what I imagine Kerry might like. The fruit is topped with cold quinoa, home made granola, and either oat milk or yogurt. I am fortunate to be able to have such pleasure in my life.

I want to write about these fruit bowls because they hold a secret about life. I'm pretty sure they do. But I need to warn you that in the writing it's going to be hard to keep things clear and well defined, definitely for me but maybe for you too. You see, there are a variety of fruits, and they're all different from each other and it's hard to tell exactly how they feel about these differences. It's also hard to tell how my thoughts and feelings about the fruits influence what the differences are. I have trouble keeping myself separate from the fruits, and there are moments when I'm not sure that we are actually separate.

Let's do our best.

The foundation on which the fruit bowl is built is apple. These days I've been getting "Pink Lady" apples. They're crisp and not too expensive. The name kind of confuses me because apples always seemed to me when I was a boy to have a kind of masculine energy. Growing up, apples were always there, long before I knew that mangoes existed or that papaya was orange. They were familiar, native to northern climates, a gift for a teacher, the thing you'd eat each day to stay healthy. Hard and hardy, always willing to show up and put a shoulder into the effort. Dependable.

Apples have a bit of an attitude problem. They think that they set the standard for fruit, that if everybody just tried harder maybe they could do it properly, like them. Their solid white flesh seems to them pretty close to the divine. They are prone to disdain for the exotic. I've had to intervene with their treatment of kiwi.

All the other fruit hate apple, at least a good portion of the time.

Baptists don't believe in mangoes, and besides which globalization hadn't yet brought them regularly to our local supermarkets, so I never ate one growing up in Saskatchewan. Then, as a freethinking adult I went Gallivanting to Trinidad and found myself trying to eat in the tidy, proper way that my dad taught me and ending up with juice up to my elbow. And, of course, all over my face. Which left me equally delighted and appalled.

Mango was the strongest flavor in the bowl this morning, which annoyed apple and left papaya feeling predictably overlooked, again. Banana was too concerned about herself to notice.

Banana is the narcissist in the group. Worried about being sterile thanks to commercialization. Grappling with whether to self-identify as an herb or fruit, as arguments can be made for either or both. And engaged in an ongoing battle with apple about which of them was plucked by Eve in the Garden. Banana is sure she owns the central spot in world fruit history.

You get the picture. How all these different fruits not only identify with their specific qualities, but compare themselves with the other fruits to try to make the case to themselves and to the larger fruit world that they are at minimum worthwhile, and probably the best.

Recently, a formal complaint was launched by strawberry, which claimed a systematic historical oppression had been perpetuated by apple, or perhaps by the demon beyond the fruit bowl (me) who was making the choices that favoured apple. Strawberry wanted to claim the right to be the foundational fruit in future bowls, despite the fact of tasting more and more like cardboard these days. Strawberry wanted past inequities addressed.

I felt shame for the ways in which strawberry's' critique struck home. For how, without my realizing it I had been complicit in promoting an apple-centric view of the fruit bowl. I started to participate in an open discussion among all the fruits about all of these problems. I have to say it was not pleasant. Maybe necessary, but definitely not pleasant. Rudeness was frequent. And, interestingly, it reminded me quite a lot of life outside the fruit bowl.

And then things got worse. Apple, feeling besieged and unhappy, piped up that everyone should quit their bickering. That after all, they were all fruit and shared the same challenges of being eaten from the same bowl.

Hoo boy! Mango had a lot of juicy things to say about that. As did all the other fruit. Their point being that apple had had a favoured role all this time, and that the suffering that was incurred was not a level playing field. Some fruits suffered more than other fruits. Which was fair enough.

The whole messy fruit bowl situation reminded me of listening to the Dalai Lama speaking about compassion. He suggested that a way to cultivate compassion for others was to imagine that every person that you meet in your life was your mother in another life. Now, I like the Dalai Lama. I more than like him, I greatly respect his wisdom and his dedication to easing suffering. But what was he thinking? I mean, I love my mom. Lots. But the thought that everyone I meet has in another life been unable to maintain proper boundaries and looked to me to provide a kind of emotional support that no kid should be expected to provide. Wow.

Sidebar: It might be that the Dalai Lama, and Tibetan Buddhism more broadly, should pay more attention to marketing. Tony Robbins would never have made that kind of gross misjudgement.

Now the Dalai Lama's intention was not to freak me or other people out. No, it was to find a way for us to experience our intimate connectedness with others. Maybe apple was trying to do the same thing. I don't think so, but maybe. More likely he was just trying to find a way to avoid acknowledging how his take on differences had made life hard for other fruit, and to also avoid the possibility that maybe he should suck it up and change his behaviour.

It would be nice if there was no need for the Dalai Lama to have to be looking for ways to remind us of our connectedness. Nice if we weren't so fiercely attached to our own sense of who we are and how we are different and better than others. And if those attachments didn't lead to all kinds of trouble in the fruit bowl and everywhere else.

But there doesn't seem to be any way around this dilemma. Once again, it does seem that we are DOOMED. We can't help but attend to differences. Indeed, it is a necessary feature of child development to become aware of being separate and different from others and also to form a working sense of identity. With this discovery kids feel empowered and able to locate themselves in the world. You know, I am this, which is different in these ways from you or from strawberry.

While it may be a necessary feature of being human to cultivate a sense of separateness, it comes at a cost. Which is to experience the outside world, the otherness out there, as a threat. And which is to lose touch with an earlier and more primal truth, that we live in connection with everything. This is especially so when everyone around us encourages us to emphasize our separate selfness and seek to get what we can for ourselves, whatever that might mean for others. Which as I understand it, is pretty much the function of family, school, and Capitalism.

> Sidebar: In consultation with the god Ethics, I feel it is important to state the following before proceeding with this argument any further. I have a vested interest in this discussion because I'd like the fruit in my bowl to be happy, as I expect that if they're happy they will taste better, be more easily digested, and I won't have to feel guilty about their poor quality of life. I am not purely altruistic. In case you were assuming I was.

What do we know about the possibilities for reducing the toxic tensions that so often result from our sense of separateness from others, and our focus on differences? Well, social psychology research shows that having contact with others can help, if the quality of that contact allows us to see beyond superficialities and stereotypes. So, for example, if apple can have a fuller experience of banana, then he is less likely to just focus on her neurotic narcissism. He can notice some of her strengths, (like her ability to cooperate flavourfully with peanut butter), and can perhaps feel some empathy for why she struggles in her particular ways. And even more importantly, the two of them may find places where they can identify shared experiences and commiserate over them. Like how they hate the texture of the yogurt when it gets slathered all over them. Or about how they wish strawberry could tone it down a bit. They can find a common bond, across differences.

This would be good. Unlikely, but good.

I'd like to be more radical about the potential for rediscovering connectedness. Like Jimi Hendrix recommended, "I'm going to wave my freak flag high!

The fruit in the fruit bowl is all made up of molecules and cells. While the configuration varies from one fruit to the next, when the fruit gets eaten by the demon, all the different molecules and cells mix together and get absorbed into the demon's own mix. We don't need to go into elimination issues here as that just complicates the central idea, which is that this idea of separateness gets a bit murky at a biological level. Who is apple inside the demon? Is the demon in any way separate from mango?

So, that's a dandy argument. Not to be lightly dismissed. But everything that we know from all the sciences and maths is that the further we push into matter, the more things fall apart. That organisms and atoms and mathematical formulas all at some point disappear into formlessness.

Ok, we are now trending into some deep shit. This is mysticism central. Where we might entertain a truth that the same vital force emanating from apple also emanates from banana and from you. Not that we should forget that apple and banana have differences, and that they should be sorted out, but to step beyond that understanding to experience what they have that is most similar. What the mystics have labeled Thusness, the Nature of Reality, the Life Force, God, and countless other terms that get us no closer to direct knowing.

So that's a cool idea.

But who cares about ideas? There are a million of them and they come and go like fashion.

How about experience? Let's veto thoughts and ideas for the moment, as they just make a lot of unnecessary noise. Could apple and banana and you and I experience the vitality that we share? If we just sat and looked at and listened to and opened our hearts, could we feel the way that we are the same?

I expect most of you will have hit the ground with a thud by now, but if you're still with me, out on this limb, then welcome to the happy DOOM experience. Where we can taste that our sense of separateness, while important in some ways, is more of an appearance than a reality. And that we need not be constrained and defined by it, and made to suffer because of it. We can be free to gallivant in the connection that can't be undone.

How's that for an ending?

Benedictus DOOMinus

May you be well

May you be happy

May you be DOOMED

Printed in Great Britain
by Amazon

86598796R00061